BIRDS

Designed by Sonia Chaghatzbanian

Library of Congress Cataloging-in-Publication Data
Martin, Gilles, 1956–
[Oiseaux. English]
Birds / photographs by Gilles Martin ; text by Philippe J. Dubois and Valérie Guidoux ; drawings by Jean Chevallier.
p. cm.
ISBN 0-8109-5878-3
1. Birds. I. Dubois, Philippe J. II. Guidoux, Valérie. III. Title.

QL673.M376 2005
598—dc22
2004022214

Printed and bound in Belgium
10 9 8 7 6 5 4 3 2 1

Harry N. Abrams, Inc.
100 Fifth Avenue
New York, NY 10011
www.abramsbooks.com

Abrams is a subsidiary of

LA MARTINIÈRE
GROUPE

BIRDS

Photographs by
Gilles Martin

Text by
Philippe J. Dubois
and Valérie Guidoux

Drawings by
Jean Chevallier

HARRY N. ABRAMS, INC., PUBLISHERS

Contents

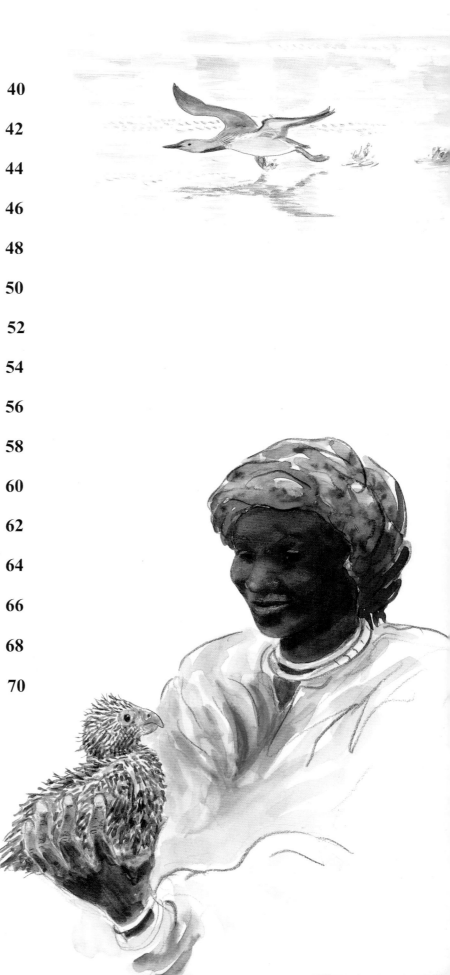

How Gilles Martin Does His Work

When you're an animal photographer, the biggest problem you face is that wild creatures do not just sit still in front of the camera.

Usually, they slip away into some hiding place. But that is exactly what Gilles Martin loves: the difficulty of lying in wait for anything that stirs, whether it's a leopard in the savannah or a small toad huddled happily in a puddle near Martin's house in France. The great thing about photographing birds is that they are spread out all over the Earth: at sea, swooping over mountains, punctuating desert silences, in tropical forests and polar regions . . . even twittering in the whispering branches of a little neighborhood park.

Martin likes to photograph animals as they go about the private routines people normally don't see. Penguins don't pose much of a problem, because they don't mind photographers visiting their nesting grounds. Usually, though, birds fear humans. So, Martin has created all kinds of paraphernalia in order to stay

hidden: He creeps along beaches beneath a sand-colored tarp, he sets up infrared cells that trigger photographs when birds such as robins land in a particular spot, and he even stalks along ponds beneath a screening contraption mounted on floats that he pushes forward.

In the floating contraption, Martin must sometimes wait, motionless and quiet, for hours. Squatting in the water in a watertight suit from 6:00 to 11:00 A.M.—that's a long, uncomfortable stretch of work! Nature lovers are patient people, though. They have to be: during just one springtime mating season, Martin spent 500 hours in his contraption in a pond in Brenne, France, photographing the processions of various birds, from the nest-building process to the raising of the young.

One day, while he was watching a grebe's nest from his contraption, Martin saw the male and female birds suddenly begin fortifying the nest at a frenetic pace. Martin wondered what was happening. Then, abruptly, the female settled on the nest, her hindquarters aimed at the photographer. She began to lay—that's what was whipping the birds into such a frantic state. The egg appeared, the female turned her head, and—*click!* This photo, which you can see on page 44, was a real "scoop," a beautiful, rare shot.

One eventful photograph can make up for all of the failures, all of the disappointments. You can easily spend long hours and get nothing in return. It is quite possible, for example, to organize a costly expedition to a river in the Amazon Basin without bringing back the photos you had hoped for.

Today, Martin travels the world photographing species threatened with extinction. Protecting birds means, first and foremost, discovering them, observing them, and learning their names and how they live. This is the essential first step that Martin's pictures encourage us to take.

This plastic goose (above) is a decoy. Mounted on a remote-controlled model boat, it attracts other species, which the photographer can then capture on film.

Birds Were Once . . . Dinosaurs?

The ostrich is the world's biggest bird. If you observe it closely, you can detect similarities with certain small dinosaurs!

W hat do a swallow and a dinosaur have in common? More than you might think.

Birds first appeared on Earth about 150 million years ago. They were the descendants of certain dinosaurs, whose scales underwent a gradual metamorphosis to become feathers. These animals then moved from **bipedalism** (that is, walking on two feet) to flight, the mysterious result of evolution. Did they start by gliding? Did they first climb trees? It is very hard to reconstruct with any certainty the story of what happened. Beyond doubt, though, a common (and unknown) ancestor produced both birds and some small dinosaurs, such as the velociraptor, which were fast predators. Fossil evidence shows that velociraptors had similarities to today's birds, such as the wishbone (formed by the fused clavicles, or collarbones), the pivoting wrist, the three toes positioned forward, and . . . feathers!

The velociraptor fairly closely resembled the **archaeopteryx**, which is held to be the ancestor of all birds. It lived around 145 million years ago.

When the dinosaurs vanished 65 million years ago, most of the present-day orders of birds already lived on Earth. They were singing long before humans were there to hear them.

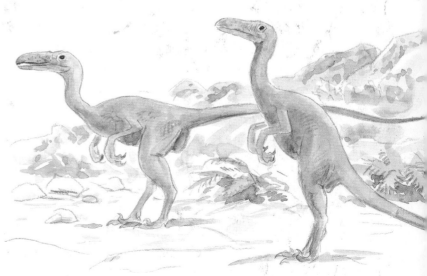

The velociraptor, which belonged to the family of the dromaeosaurs, looked a bit like the birds of our own era.

Let Diversity Reign!

The Toco Toucan (scientific name: *Ramphastos toco*) is famous for its extraordinary beak, which, though enormous, weighs very little. People say "the toucan," but there are currently at least 40 species of toucans!

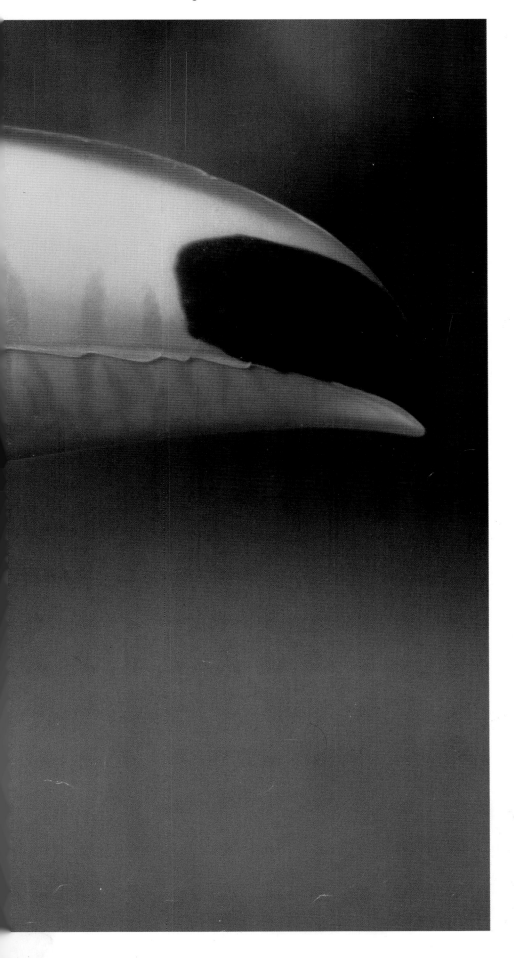

Over the millions of years that separate us from the dinosaurs, birds evolved and took on an extraordinary diversity of features. Some species appeared and vanished naturally; more recently, though, others have perished at the hands of humans.

Today, we know of 9,900 species of birds, and we're discovering a few new ones every year, mainly in tropical forests.

Birds inhabit every possible setting, from the vast ice reaches of Antarctica through hot deserts to the highest mountain peaks. Adaptation to each of these environments means that birds display a dazzling range of sizes, colors, and shapes.

For poetry lovers, bird names resonate exotically, magically: the Cream-colored Courser, the Woodlark, the Demoiselle Crane, and the Goldcrest. Each bird also has a Latin name, fashioned of two parts, which enables **ornithologists**, scientists who study birds, to understand one another throughout the world when they're talking about the same bird.

On the island of Hawaii, around 30 species of birds belong to the family Drepanidinae. Their differing beaks are adapted for getting food from various sources.

Creatures of the Air

The elongated feathers of the White-tailed Tropicbird's tail create a graceful contour in the sky. Its wings flap rapidly, an example of beating flight.

How are flying birds able to defy gravity and air resistance?

First, their light skeletons give them an advantage. Some of their bones are hollow, constructed of a system of crosswalls, like the internal struts of an airplane, that give substantial strength. Also, flight requires a great deal of energy: Birds use powerful **pectoral muscles** to support the beating of their wings. Their respiratory systems work at very high, efficient levels, and flexible but strong **thoracic ribcages**—the system of bones protecting the chest—prevent wing motion from compressing the chest. Because of this, lungs cannot expand each time air is breathed in; instead, they are connected with air sacs located throughout the body, which also reduce the bird's weight and act as insulation. A bird's heart is an especially effective pump that, even in the smallest sparrow, beats at nearly 500 pulses per minute. When you consider that human hearts beat about 70 pulses per minute, you begin to appreciate the incredible amount of energy that birds use in order to fly.

Finally, of course, feathers, which are light and arranged in patterns, are a wonderful tool for beating the air and gliding.

Some birds take off directly from a standing position. Others, such as the albatross, need a running start to gather speed.

Light as a Feather

This variegated gannet displays its feathers in all of their diversity. They have marvelous colors and shapes, and even when tinted in dark, somber tones, the feathers are patterned in beautiful motifs.

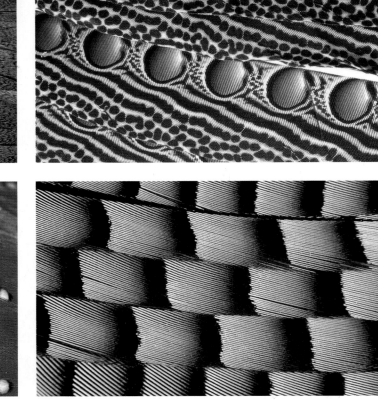

A remarkable device, the feather, allows birds to fly. There are two main kinds of feathers. **Down** helps maintain body heat. It covers fledglings, then, later on, remains hidden beneath the large feathers of the adult. **Contour** are the shaped feathers; they are both a bird's "costume" and its flight tool.

Contour feathers differ depending on function. The **remiges** bordering the wings allow flight. When the bird flaps its wings, these feathers push the air downward and to the rear. The covering feathers protect the bird from cold and water. Then, finally, the tail feathers—the **rectrices**—stabilize flight more or less as a rudder does. They also aid in stopping. In some birds, such as the snipe, the rectrices can vibrate when the birds fly during the mating season, producing a kind of quavering sound. In this case, they produce the male's "song," which attracts the female.

Feathers make up an impenetrable, warm dress that protects the bird. In turn, the bird must clean and oil its feathers using a special gland, since the slightest stain (or the greatest, such as those caused by oil spills at sea) will damage this vital covering.

The interwoven **barbs** and smaller, connecting **barbules** make the feather effective for flight and protection.

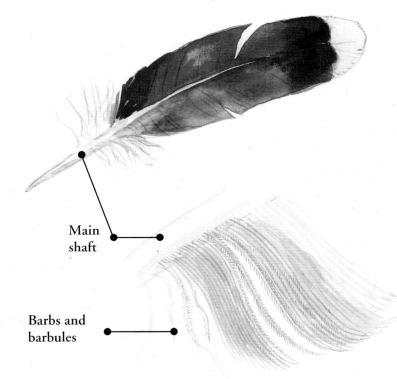

Main shaft

Barbs and barbules

Costume Changes

These Black-headed (or Laughing) Gulls on a pond in central France sport their wedding plumage. During mating season, they have handsome dark hoods.

Birds' colors change over the course of their lifetimes. At the beginning, colors change when the fledging develops feathers over its down. The young of some species wear plumage that is quite different from the one they'll have as adults. This is true of seagulls, which, although brown during their first three years of life, become white and gray thereafter.

During a bird's entire life span, feathers deteriorate and get replaced at a pace that varies depending on the species. This costume change is called **molting**. During this stage, which may last from a few days to a few months, the bird replaces all or a part of its feathers.

Molting normally occurs twice every year. Usually springtime is the beginning of the mating season, when many birds put on their beautiful mating plumage in order to attract a partner. Once the young birds have grown, another molting stage brings back the winter plumage, which typically has darker, more understated colors. In the case of the Black-headed, or Laughing Gull, only the head changes color. However, in the Common Redstart and other species, the bird's entire plumage varies from one season to another.

The Black-headed Gull loses its dark hood in winter.

Young Herring gulls have brown plumage. In adult birds, the head is entirely white, except in winter.

As the Crow (and the Crane, and the Owl, and the Goose . . .) Flies

Because wings have a convex shape on the top, air passes more rapidly over the top than it does underneath. This creates a difference in lift, so a bird that beats its wings, such as the Japanese crane, below left, will not fall from the sky. The Marsh Harrier, below right, is preparing for a landing, the wings and tail spread, the claws extended to absorb the impact.

Cranes perform flapping (or powered) flight; that is, they fly by continuously, rapidly beating their wings. Ducks and geese do the same thing, and they're joined by most of the **Passeriformes** (perching birds). On the other hand, some larger species, storks and pelicans for instance, travel by soaring. These heavier birds can save energy by using warm air currents to rise up in the sky. They let themselves be carried and they soar, gradually losing altitude as they look for other thermal updrafts to climb again. Seabirds similarly make use of airflows created by waves to spring forward above swells. There are still other forms of flight, too, such as the stationary flight of hummingbirds, which feed on flower nectar. These small birds can even fly backward!

In all of these cases, flight gives birds amazing freedom of movement. They fly to look for food, to escape predators, to migrate, and so on. Free to travel wherever they please, birds have discovered and settled in every part of the globe.

Not surprisingly, takeoff is excellent protection against land-based predators.

Not Everyone Can Fly

The wings of King Penguins are actually powerful flippers, which allow the birds to glide underwater like fish. Their short, dense plumage protects them from the cold, as though they were wearing a diver's wet suit.

Penguins are the best known of **apterous**, or wingless, birds. They live in the Antarctic and feed in the ocean. Evolution has transformed their wings into true flippers, allowing them to fish at great depths the way dolphins do.

Other apterous birds walk or run. These include the emu, the rhea, and, of course, the ostrich, the fastest runner of the bird world, which can reach speeds of up to 45 miles per hour! Contrary to what you might think, these birds have actually benefited from their inability to fly, because they can take advantage of food on the ground that other species neglect. On the other hand, an increasingly hostile environment makes survival difficult for certain apterous species, including some small birds on islands in the Pacific and Indian Oceans. Rails, which resemble moorhens, have nearly lost the ability to fly simply because, for thousands of years, they inhabited a predator-free habitat. Then, during the eighteenth century, humans swarmed these islands, bringing with them packs of rats, pigs, cats, and other animals. Flightless birds suddenly became easy targets. Many, such as the dodo of Reunion Island, vanished quickly.

The kiwi cannot fly, having only stumps for wings. It feeds on land.

Beaks: Tools for Every Job

Short-toed Eagle

Variegated Cormorant

Grand Eclectus

Sacred Ibis of Aldabra

Gannet

A beak may sometimes be extremely beautiful, but it's not there just for decoration. First and foremost, it is a precision instrument used for feeding.

Inca Tern

Pink Flamingo

Northern Raven

A bird searches for food with its beak. Since each species has its own special diet, the beak is shaped accordingly. Does the bird have to tear to pieces, peck, capture in flight, grind, store, dig up, or even filter its food? Well, there's a beak for every job.

Raptors have hooked beaks that enable them to tear their prey apart, while the beak of the cormorant, also hooked and sharp, allows it to catch and hold fish. The hooked beak of the parrot is even stronger than the raptor's, since it has to pierce the shells of huge nuts. Flamingoes use their beaks as filters to trap (or skim) algae from the silt-strewn waters of coastlines. Woodpeckers pock tree bark with their beaks, steely and straight, to flush out the invertebrates they eat.

Of course, beaks have other uses, too. They are used to smooth out feathers, for cleaning, sometimes for fighting, for carrying nesting materials, and for gaping wide when the bird projects its cry or song.

Pelicans store fish for their young in the enormous pouch in their beak.

What's on the Menu?

The Yellow-billed Hornbill of tropical Africa holds a huge locust in its beak. In just a few seconds, the insect will find itself in the bird's stomach.

What's on the menu? Well, that depends on the species. Birds take full advantage of nature's abundance, and the greatest number of them feed on plants. Among these, **granivores** (grain eaters), such as the chaffinch and the sparrow, eat mainly seeds. Birds that favor fruits, like some pigeons, toucans, and numerous tropical species, are said to be **frugivorous**. **Herbivorous** species, such as geese, feed on leaves and grass.

Among the **carnivores**, birds that hunt small invertebrates, like the swallow, are more commonly called **insectivores**. The term "carnivore" is usually used for birds that, like the raptors, feed on large animals (rodents, birds, reptiles, etc.). Then, finally, we come to the crows, rooks, and ravens, which, since they eat pretty much anything, are called **omnivores**.

Some species change their diet as the seasons progress. The Blackcap, an insectivore when the weather's pleasant, eats fruits and berries in autumn and winter. On the other hand, the insectivores that have to stick to the same menu, like the swallow, must fly south for the winter to hunt for insects, since they can no longer find enough to eat if they remain where it's cold.

Geese graze on grass, as do sheep. They can also eat seeds and berries.

The kestrel feeds on small rodents.

The Night Shift

The Great Gray Owl, left, and the barn owl, right, hunt small rodents at night with the aid of their extraordinary hearing. The disk of feathers surrounding their face acts like a **parabola** which funnels sound into the ear openings.

The large majority of birds are active during the day; they're called **diurnal**. Those that feed at night, while the others sleep, are called **nocturnal**. Among these, owls are the most widely known.

Owls have all of the gear they need to carry out their nighttime rounds. First of all, their primary wing feathers have frayed edges that muffle the sound of the air rushing over the wing surface, allowing the owl to fly silently. Owls also possess acute night vision, and, above all, sensitive hearing. Their auditory canals are arranged to heighten sound capture, including noises that our ears cannot pick up. Incredibly, the Snowy Owl (a large white owl that lives in the Arctic) can pinpoint a field mouse beneath the snow and catch it "blind."

Other birds, such as the nighthawk, feed on insects at night. Also, among small wading birds, or gulls, we find some that are active mainly at night. This lets them avoid competition with other, closely-related species that live in the same space during the day.

In the middle of the night, snipe probe silt with their long beaks. They catch small invertebrates simply by groping "blindly."

Predator Birds Are Terribly . . . Useful?

A Steller's Sea Eagle lands on a block of ice in the Sea of Japan. It hunts and eats fish. A less intimidating–looking bird, the Red-backed Shrike, also makes a fearsome predator.

The Steller's Sea Eagle is a fish-eating predator. In the waters of its territory, carnivorous fish eat herbivorous fish (the most numerous group) that feed on aquatic plants—a food chain composed of hunters and their prey.

In every environment, predators play a very important role: they prevent the overpopulation of other species, growth that, in the predators' absence, would disrupt the natural balance. Just think of how many mice and voles, for example, there would be if not for raptors! At the same time, the number of predators must remain low in any single environment; otherwise, there wouldn't be enough herbivores. Balance, then, is the key. Predator birds raise only one or two young, and rarely more than that, which helps keep the balance in check. Some predators, such as the albatross, don't nest every year. Raptors also don't reproduce before the age of three or four years, while small birds grow to adulthood in just a few months. However, some raptors live a long life, sometimes up to a few decades.

Big raptors are not the only predators, though. Some sparrows are ferocious hunters. That's certainly true of the shrike, which can seize prey as big as itself: field mice, lizards, or even other small birds.

Raptors feed mainly on small rodents.

After digesting, raptors **regurgitate** balls of fur, feathers, and bones of their prey in the form of pellets.

The Art of Self-Defense

The jackal pictured below has come upon the shelter of a Crowned Crane's chicks. One of the parents spreads wide its wings to intimidate the enemy. Faced with such a display, the jackal will ultimately give up.

The kingdom of birds has victims as well as predators. A single species may be a predator . . . then become prey. The swallow, which eats insects, may fall prey to the hawk, which may then be targeted by the nighttime attack of an Eagle Owl.

Constant vigilance is a bird's best protection against predators. When enemies approach, birds emit warning cries that do not sound like their usual song, prompting everyone to scatter. However, birds have also devised tricks for when an enemy attacks them or their young. Chicks prove, in fact, to be easy targets: even though their down often camouflages them in surrounding vegetation, they emit a smell that can alert predators. When this happens, adult birds do not hesitate to place themselves between predator and chick, either by exaggerated displays of strength (as shown here by the crowned crane), or, at the opposite end of the scale, by feigning weakness. For example, the Ringed Plover stumbles away, pretending to have a broken wing, in order to draw a predator's attention away from its young.

Finally, birds often congregate to chase away an enemy. When it's pursued by a squadron of dozens of birds, a hawk will hunt elsewhere.

The hobby charges at its prey: swallows, beetles, and dragonflies.

Dressing for Light and Shade

The vividly-colored Quetzal, right, with its incandescent plumage might seem designed to attract attention. And yet, its luminous appearance hides it as effectively in its environment as the lackluster plumage of the reddish-brown anhinga (also known as the Oriental Darter), left, does in its own.

The anhinga and the Quetzal teach us the surprising powers of color. Whether unassuming and wan or brilliant and vivid, colors let a bird show or conceal itself. The Oriental Darter, perched on a piece of deadwood to dry its feathers, disappears into its environment, thereby hiding from predators while at the same time hunting unsuspecting fish. Not only is it dressed in different shades of brown, but lines running horizontally in its plumage break up the bird's silhouette. The anhinga holds itself in a posture that makes it seem to be merely a part of the background. In fact, the bird's complete motionlessness is the best possible camouflage, since movement is usually what betrays an animal's presence.

Vividly colored birds do not necessarily stand out any more than drab ones. The Golden Oriole with its brilliant yellow plumage lives in the treetops. There, among the twinkling patches of shade and sun vibrating on the leaves, only a practiced eye can make out the bird. The same contrasting light effect conceals the quetzal in its home forests.

The colors of male birds also serve to attract their partners. Females, on the other hand, usually have a dull coloration, enabling some species to nest unnoticed in open ground.

The female eider tends her eggs out in the open, where she is hidden by coloring that mimics her surroundings.

Sing Out, Sing Loud

The Cock of the Rock, below left, and the cassowary have an especially spectacular appearance—but, alas, without the songs to match.

Bird songs carry meaning. In most cases, males are the ones who sing. Usually they sing, "This is my territory. I'm here, it's my home, and all other males can scram." Singing can also attract females.

Each species has its own song, and although humans may have difficulty identifying the differences, each individual male has his own special song too. Studies have shown that among birds of the same species, those with the most elaborate songs have the best chances of seducing a mate. Interestingly enough, song is not innate. Males learn to sing starting in their youth, listening to their father (or other males). Some birds, such as the starling, have a cracked, dissonant voice; however, they can compensate by imitating the songs of other birds. They use this trick to expand their repertoire.

The nightingale and the song thrush are true virtuosos, even though their plumage is fairly drab. On the other hand, very handsome birds often possess mediocre voices.

The Great Reed Warbler, with its unspectacular plumage, sits singing on a reed. Its powerful, rasping song will ultimately attract a female.

The Art of Display

The male frigate bird (a seabird) has a red pouch on its neck, which inflates like a balloon, while the peacock spreads its tail of shimmering feathers before its future mate.

Courtship display is a kind of ballet that the male performs (sometimes with the female's participation) in order to charm his partner. Nearly all bird species enact some kind of courtship, sometimes with song.

But for those birds that will never become the singing idol of the **avian** kingdom, courtship's visual displays become highly elaborate. Great-crested Grebes, for example, salute each other face to face, bowing and shaking hundreds of times with their heads and necks, their feathered crowns fanned and extended. Other birds, such as the peacock, use their richly colored plumage to attract females. The bird of paradise, adorned with its radiant feathers, does not stop at being beautiful; it also launches into acrobatic maneuvers in the treetops.

Once these performances have proved successful, the male mounts the female, and each spreads its feathers apart to clear away an area called the **cloaca**. Coupling lasts for a few seconds only, during which the birds are positioned cloaca to cloaca.

While geese and jackdaws choose mates for their entire lives, most species change partners every mating season. It even happens that a single male courts several females at once, and that females let themselves be courted by several males simultaneously.

To aid in the display, these different male warriors play at ferocious—but never deadly—combat.

Beware! This Is My Territory!

These two male common (or Eurasian) coots use their beaks and feet to fight—but they will not get injured. They are quarreling over territorial boundaries.

As with many animals, birds are territorial, defending their areas with the most ferocity during mating season, when they pair off in couples and raise their young. A blackbird living in a garden is the master of a well-defined part of it, and he will not tolerate the presence of any other male in his area. This territorial instinct, the strength of which grows or diminishes depending on the species and the male's experience, vanishes once mating season ends. At that point, each bird can come and go as it pleases.

The size of a territory is often linked to the size of the species. Thus, the territory of a blackbird may be several dozens of square yards large, while the domain of the golden eagle may stretch over several dozen square miles. As for species that live in colonies, their individual territories may not extend beyond their nests. This is true for the gannet, the penguin, and the guillemot, whose nests are packed tightly together on steep seaside cliffs.

When raising their young, Arctic terns attack any intruder wandering into their territory.

Strength in Numbers

Queleas, or Red-billed Weaverbirds, are small birds resembling sparrows that live in large groups on the African savannas. They can ravage a millet field in no time.

Birds that live in groups are said to have the herd instinct, as do queleas, which gather in crowds throughout the year. It's a lifestyle that has its advantages. First of all, finding sources of food is easier when a lot of individuals are looking for them. Also, a solitary bird runs a much greater chance of being caught by a raptor or carnivorous mammal than does an individual living in an intimidating group. Young birds have a much better chance of survival in a flock. When geese gather in large groups for the winter, families stay together. As a result, the young benefit not only from the security of group living, but also learn under the care of their parents.

Many birds live in groups only at certain times. There are many species that, like gulls and starlings, typically tend to scatter at daybreak but congregate at night. This nighttime gathering lets individuals keep warm, more easily evade predators, and slip one another clues about the most promising feeding grounds. Still other species assemble once mating is over (starlings and crows, for instance), while seabirds flock together in the spring to nest.

A group of starlings in flight huddles together in a ball at the sight of a sparrowhawk, which will then have more trouble picking out a single bird.

Nesting in Colonies

Painted storks reproduce while living in colonies. Some species of large wading birds, such as herons and egrets, also nest in this way.

Many seabirds (guillemots, puffins, gulls, and others) tend to the propagation of their species while nesting in colonies. Lone wanderers the rest of the year, they gather in spring by the thousands on small islands in the sea or on cliffs rising over the coastline, where a number of different species rub wings. For a few months, these places become wildly animated scenes: weaving up, away and back, crisscrossing flight paths, the commotion of calls and cries. Then the season ends, and the grounds are left deserted, scattershot with droppings.

Birds that nest in colonies mount a better defense against predators; there is always someone around to sound the alarm. Adults work in relays in their quest for food, and information gets passed around quickly among the colony's members. Some species gather the fledglings in the creche, or nursery, where they are looked after by a few adults. The others can then dine in peace. Pink flamingoes follow this pattern.

But great hordes of birds can also pose problems. A colony attracts more predators than does a single, well-concealed nest. And then, if an accident occurs, such as a pollution spill, habitat destruction, or an epidemic disease, a large number of birds may die in a single stroke.

Lappet-faced Vultures nest in pairs. However, they meet up with others around the carcasses on which they feed.

The Master Builders

The Seychelles Paradise-Flycatcher builds its nest, made of plant fibers and grasses, in the fork of a branch. The White Tern simply sticks its single egg in a tree.

For most birds, building the nest—the shelter for eggs and the refuge of the fledglings—is a matter of great importance. They patiently gather and assemble the materials for the nest, whether it's a pile of twigs and branches made by a magpie, or an extremely elaborate affair, like the nest of the Common Tailor bird, which uses its beak to sew two leaves together with plant fibers. Occasionally these light structures are durable enough to last for years, provided a few repairs are made every spring.

Each species adapts to its environment. Accordingly, Great-crested Grebes make nests that float in ponds, while kingfishers dig burrows into the banks of streams. In the hot lands of Oceania, **megapodes** bury their eggs to keep them warm.

One final requirement: the nest must be invisible. It is often hidden among vegetation, and it is sometimes completely enclosed on itself to better hide the eggs from potential predators. Or, just as discreetly, it may simply be scratched out at ground level, where the female hatches her eggs beneath the vigilant gaze of the male.

In Australia, the gardener bird adorns its nest with found objects, such as seeds, flowers, glass beads, bones, shells, or plastic fragments.

Breaking Away . . . From Your Egg

Like all birds, the Black-necked Grebe lays its eggs through the same opening from which its droppings pass. The fledgling takes shape inside the egg; it must then break open the shell, as this little herring gull is doing.

All birds lay eggs. After coupling and fertilization, an egg forms in the female's womb, then it is laid in the nest. Generally speaking, an entire day passes between the laying of two eggs. Once all are laid (from one to as many as ten eggs!), the female, and sometimes the male, sits on them to keep them warm. Depending on the species, **incubation** can last anywhere from ten to twenty-eight days. During this interval, the embryo develops, drawing nourishment from the food stored in the egg itself.

The fledgling must be able to free itself from the egg in order to be born. Using a sharp projection called the **egg tooth**, which has formed on the beak, it breaks the shell. The egg tooth disappears shortly after birth.

When they hatch, young birds are almost fully developed. **Nidicolous** fledglings are those fledglings that are born featherless and blind (tits and eagles, for example). They need several days before they can open their eyes and become covered with down. Their parents feed them until they can fly off. **Nidifugous** chicks, those that leave the nest almost immediately, are born covered with down, and can feed themselves. They waddle off after their parents only a few hours after hatching.

Egg colors and shapes differ according to species.

Squatters and Spongers

The young gray cuckoo shown is trying to shove an egg over the side. He wants the comfort of the nest for himself! Oxpeckers, on the other hand, don't disturb anybody. They are getting rid of (eating) tiny creatures that have gotten into the giraffe's coat.

The female cuckoo does not incubate her eggs; instead, she tricks adults of other species to do her work for her. She deposits her egg in another nest, right in the midst of those of another bird's. That bird will then hatch the cuckoo's egg with the same devotion that she would lavish on her own. How is it possible for parents to make such a huge blunder? Well, the cuckoo's egg is the same color as those of the species whose homes cuckoos normally invade, making it less noticeable. The cuckoo baby normally hatches before the other chicks, and the first thing it does is kick out the other eggs. The adoptive parents find that their newly hatched chick is much bigger than they expected (and even bigger than the adults themselves!), and they have to use up a lot of energy just to feed the little interloper.

In many other cases, **parasitism** (that is, the act of living at another creature's expense) may involve a kind of reciprocal arrangement. The African Oxpecker feeds by catching small insects in the coats of herbivores like the giraffe. This exchange of favors is called **commensalism**.

The Tengmalm's Owl raises its young in an old hole that was dug out, then abandoned, by a pileated woodpecker.

47

Growing Up with Mom and Dad

Chicks of the Mute Swan quickly learn how to swim and feed. Despite their skill, the young return to their parents' nest to seek tranquility and to sleep at night.

Unlike insects and **batrachians** (frogs and toads), whose young are left to their own devices from hatching time onward, young birds are lavished with the attention of their parents, who feed them, ward off predators, and in some species, teach them to migrate. Parents of nidicolous fledglings feed their young for several weeks in the nest; the fledglings consume the equivalent of their own weight in food each day. But nest-bound birds cannot escape or hide, so they are easy prey. That is why the nests of nidiculous birds are often well concealed.

Nidifugous chicks, on the other hand, leave the nest shortly after hatching and can feed by themselves. For example, a young loon can dive merely a day or two after birth, and a small pheasant can quickly locate the seeds it needs to thrive. Even still, their parents protect them for several weeks or even months.

In general, both parents bear the responsibility of rearing their chicks. In some species of ducks and wading birds, however, a single adult, in most cases the female, receives this assignment. Among gallinules (or moorhens) and bee-eaters, the young from an earlier brood may sometimes help their parents raise a new crop of chicks.

Nidicolous fledglings are born featherless and blind. About eighteen days after hatching, they are able to leave the nest.

On One's Own for Life

This young King Penguin has to nourish itself. It draws on its fat reserves until the time it learns to fish on its own. This young White spoonbill, below, will fly off from the nest at about six weeks of age.

Every bird leaves its parents someday to survive alone. Doing so usually involves two momentous trials: takeoff and the search for food.

An eaglet that has grown up on the ledge of a cliff must launch itself into the void on its first takeoff. A few days before, the young bird begins strengthening its muscles by flapping its wings in the nest and hopping between branches. Once airborne, the eaglet must capture its prey without help. Among some species, adults and their offspring stay together for a while even after the young have become fully capable of surviving on their own. Greylag geese, for example, spend their first winter as members of a family.

Other birds have a fat reserve to get through the critical time when their parents stop feeding them. For example, young Northern Gannets can manage for a few weeks while eating little or nothing; after that, it's "get along by yourself . . . or die."

But even with careful rearing and much preparation, many young birds die when they gain their freedom. Because of their inexperience, they can easily fall victim to hunger or predators.

For their first flight, barnacle geese must jump off the cliff where they were born.

Few insects are available in wintertime. Great-spotted Woodpeckers survive the season by searching for small insects and larvae underneath the bark of trees. Great tits, insect feeders in summer, eat seeds during cold and snow.

In cold and temperate regions, winter is hard for birds. Food is scarce. Beginning in autumn, many varieties of birds, the **migratory** species, fly to warmer climates. But others, called **sedentary**, endure the winter in the same place. These species can find food during the entire course of the year. Most of them are granivores (feeding on seeds and grains), and they include chaffinches and some larks. Others are omnivores, that is, birds like crows and starlings that eat pretty much anything. Insectivores may also stay. While there is little chance they will catch a gnat in midflight, they know how to dig up a few tiny creatures wriggling in their lairs.

However, when winter rages and storms, even sedentary birds must head south or face hunger. Many do not survive.

When winter eventually turns to springtime, these sedentary species begin their great task: mating and reproduction. These birds can devote more time to this than the migratory birds, which must travel long distances to get back to their nesting sites.

In winter, Long-tailed Tits ruffle their feathers and huddle against one another for warmth.

Migration Means Travel, Both Near and Far

In summer, these Bar-tailed Godwits nest in the Siberian Arctic. After migrating along the coastlines of Europe and Africa, they end up in Mauritania, where they spend the warm summers. They'll return along the same route the following spring.

Swallows are one of many species of birds to leave Europe in the fall. Nearly half of the species living on that continent nest (and reproduce) in one region, then pass the winter in another. Twice a year, in spring and autumn, they make the voyage between their two homes. This kind of trek is called **migration**. As summer winds down, the disappearing food supply and colder weather drive these birds to milder climates. Some travel over thousands of miles, others only dozens. Most of the migratory birds in the Northern Hemisphere head south. Others fly from east to west, like the rook and the starling, which leave Russia to ride out the winter season in France. In mountainous areas, birds that nest in high altitudes in summer (the Water Pipit, Wallcreeper, and others) pass the cold season in the plains below.

One obvious question, though: Why don't migratory birds stay all year in the warm-weather climates where they spend their winters? Well, if everyone nested in one location, there would be too many of them! In springtime, migratory species take advantage of the abundant food supply available in cooler climates.

A robin observed nesting in a garden during the year may not always be the same individual. Robins that nest in spring leave for the south in autumn. Another bird arriving from colder regions may then take its place.

To the Sun!

In winter, pink flamingoes that nest around ponds and lakes of the Camargue region of France migrate to areas along the rim of the Mediterranean. Some travel even farther south into Africa.

Many bird species winter in the Tropics. This is especially true of insect-feeders (swallows, warblers, and others), raptors (honey buzzards and black kites), and small wading birds, to keep from starving. In these tropical countries, these birds find a wealth of insects, whose populations fall dramatically at home in winter.

Migratory birds must cross mountains, seas, and deserts. They have to face many dangers—and most certainly exhaustion. In fact, one-half of swallows may perish during their two annual journeys.

Birds navigate by the sun, the stars, geographical features, and most probably, too, by smells and air currents. They travel most often in groups, each one of which follows a very precise route. White storks keep to the land, avoiding vast stretches of water, then cross the Mediterranean over the Straits of Gibraltar. Northern Pintails, on the other hand, do not hesitate to pass over uninterrupted water for two days at a time.

For swallows, the trek across the Sahara can mean a trip with no return.

Winter Visitors

Soaring in from the tundra of the Arctic, these Whooper Cranes spend wintertime in the warmer zone around the lakes of Western and Central Europe. On occasion, a cold spell may push them farther south.

In the coldest periods of winter, temperate regions such as Western Europe, abandoned by migratory species for Africa, become the refuge of swans and geese fleeing the Arctic. These birds live in the tundra, which in summer is carpeted with flowers and filled with the cries of chicks. In winter, though, frost and ice make searching for food very difficult. Many species of the Arctic then move southward: geese, ducks, cranes, some of the birds of prey, small waders, and many Passeriformes (perching birds) such as the Snow Bunting and Lapland Bunting. They travel several hundreds or thousands of miles until they find open water unclogged with ice and land without snow.

These birds return north after February, when the temperature slowly starts to warm up. The birds travel in stages, and most will not reach the tundra before late May, when the snow has virtually vanished. Then, they have to hurry to raise their young, since the far northern summer lasts little more than three months.

Geese fly in V- or W-shaped formations. Birds in the rear are protected by those in front.

How Birds Are Studied

The Grey Heron is a bizarre kind of migratory bird: some individuals are almost completely sedentary, while others winter in the Tropics. By attaching bands to birds, scientists are learning more and more about migration.

Banding is the attachment of a metal ring (bearing a serial number or alphabetic code and organization name) to a bird's foot. This allows scientists to better understand the routes taken by birds as they migrate. In the field, an ornithologist tracking a banded bird uses her telescope to record the numbers or letters, which she then sends to an organization that, in turn, transmits the information to researchers. Over the course of the last century, this method made it possible to learn and map out the migratory routes of most bird species living in the Northern Hemisphere. Today, scientists can use more sophisticated means: for example, an Argos beacon (a satellite transmitter) attached to a large bird enables satellites to track it with incredible accuracy during all of its travels.

Ornithologists study sedentary birds, too. To learn about all of the steps involved in the propagation of a particular species, one researcher can spend hundreds of hours making observations in the field, then almost as many at his computer entering and interpreting the data he has gathered.

Birds are caught in a mist net spread across a field, then measured, examined, weighed, banded, and released.

Protecting Habitats

On this island where thousands of Sooty Terns nest, this man is collecting eggs to eat, threatening the broods of dozens of pairs.

Animal survival depends on the natural habitats that shelter them. Today, however, many of these habitats are in peril. Large numbers of birds suffer from the deforestation of tropical woodlands, all the more alarming because 90 percent of the world's animal and plant diversity is found there. Everywhere, hedges cut down to enlarge farmland perimeters, drained marshlands, forests plundered for the lumber industry, and steppes transformed into wheat- and cornfields mean devastation that threatens animal life.

It's not enough, though, to simply stop destroying natural environments; they need to be protected from disturbances. Heavy human activity can compromise the healthy growth of young broods by introducing predators (dogs, for example), or by making the search for food more problematic. Many beaches that once provided food and shelter to shore birds like terns and plovers are now overrun by summer vacationers, with the result that some of these species are gradually slipping into extinction.

Natural parks and reserves protect these threatened habitats. Their existence is essential for allowing future generations the opportunity to admire the beauty of birds.

To enlarge farm fields, people have cut down hedges that once sheltered a large variety of birds.

Sea Wanderers in Danger

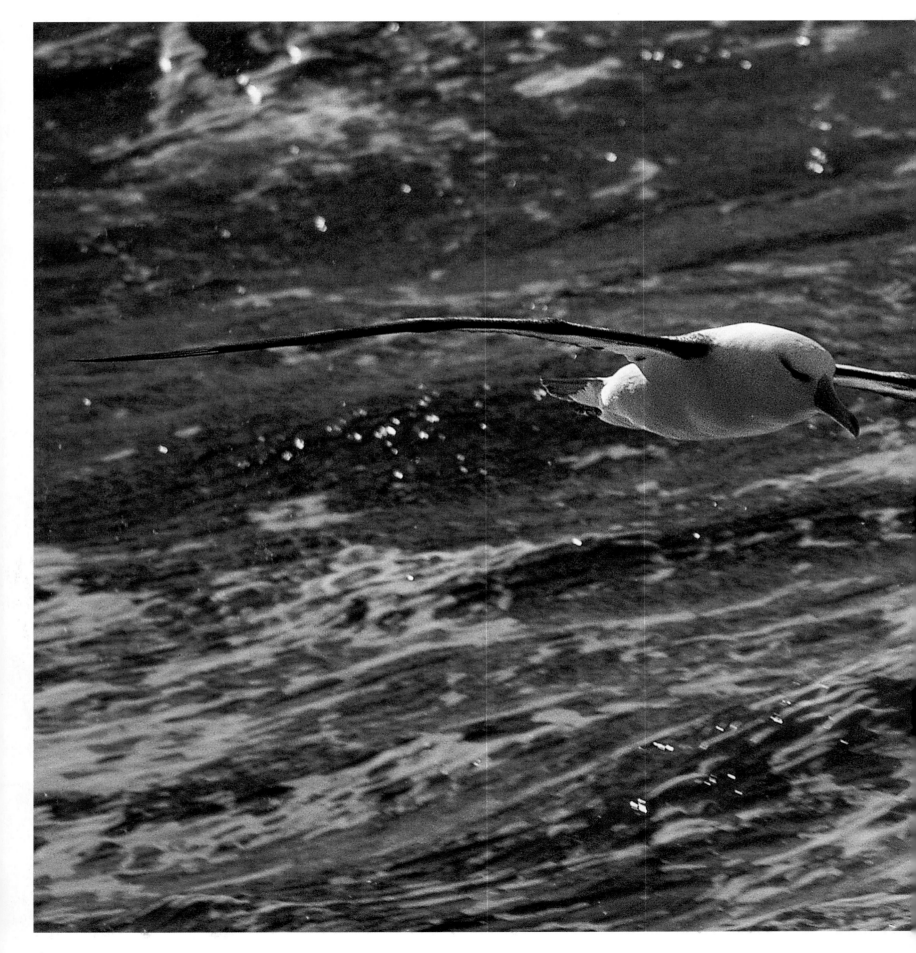

In full control as it skims, darts, and lifts above the waves in the Southern Hemisphere, this black-browed Albatross playfully maneuvers through wind and water.

For a few years now, the albatross has become a distressing symbol of our dying oceans. Indeed, virtually every species of albatross faces extinction—all because industrial fishing operations use gigantic nets barbed with hooks that these huge birds ingest when they feed. They die drowning. Not only, then, do these industrial fishing expeditions take too many fish, they also kill many birds and marine mammals, such as dolphins, which become ensnared in the nets.

Seabirds are among the first victims of marine pollution. The greatest examples of this pollution, of course, are oil spills, such as those caused by tankers such as the *Erika*, the *Exxon Valdez*, and the *Prestige*. Furthermore, the daily draining of on-board fuel tanks of ships, which releases fuel residues into ocean water, continues despite legal prohibitions. When birds settle on the affected water, oil penetrates through their plumage, causing it to lose its impermeability. The birds then die of cold or are poisoned, since they ingest the oil as they try to clean themselves. A small proportion of oil-soaked birds die on the shoreline—it's hard to calculate the numbers that die at sea.

This oil-soaked guillemot will be cared for. But if it has already ingested some oil, there is little chance it will survive.

Protecting Birds

Hunted for both its feathers and its meat, the Victoria crowned pigeon, a pigeon that inhabits Papua New Guinea, is an endangered species that needs protection.

In our time, it is estimated that nearly 1,200 species of birds (out of the 9,900 living on the planet) are threatened with extinction unless something is done to save them. That means 12 percent of all known species of birds!

For some birds, it is too late. The dodo of Reunion Island and the Carolina Parakeet of North America are two famous extinct species. Yet, how many die out without much notice? In France, more than one hundred species are threatened, such as Bonelli's Eagle of which only several pairs survive in the region of Provence. Even among common species, numbers are falling. The House Martin finds fewer and fewer buildings that are suitable for its nest.

Protecting birds means, above all, protecting bird habitats and restricting pollution. This means protecting humans, too, since we cannot live in an environment of devastation. It also means that each of us must be willing, every day, to live with animals in our neighborhood; the planet is not home to humans alone.

A number of organizations protect the black parrot of the Seychelles by providing hatching boxes in which the parrots can reproduce.

Human and Bird

A few decades ago in France, some people were still nailing barn owls to barn doors to ward off evil. Fourteen thousand years ago, Australian Aborigines drew these land birds on the walls of a cave.

As with nature in general, humans often have a strange relationship with birds. At times, a feeling of affection prompts people to offer protection, or even to cage birds for their beauty and song. On other occasions, humans hunt birds not only to feed themselves, but also, unfortunately, for entertainment. Thankfully, no one nails owls to barn doors anymore to keep evil spirits at bay, and nocturnal birds of prey enjoy complete protection.

We must remember that despite being more ancient than humans, birds evolved alongside us. They should remain, in our eyes, the symbols of grace, freedom, and peace that they have always been. It is up to us to ensure that they remain this way. As a start, we need only take time to wander with a pair of binoculars to observe them closely.

Japanese cranes were once on the verge of extinction on the island of Hokkaido. Now protected, these beautiful birds are flourishing.

Glossary

Apterous: Lacking wings. Refers to birds that do not fly.

Archaeopteryx: Literally "ancient wing," this feathered animal flourished during the Late Jurassic period, about 150 million years ago, and is widely considered to be the oldest known bird.

Avian: Relating to, or characteristic of, birds.

Barbs: The branches that extend off each side of the main shaft of a feather.

Barbules: The smaller branches that extend from the feather barbs. The interlocking barbules hold the feather shaft intact.

Batrachian: Refers to the group of land or semiaquatic amphibians that lack tails but have long hindlegs used for leaping (such as toads and frogs).

Bipedalism: The ability to walk on two legs.

Carnivore: Organism that eats meat.

Cloaca: The single opening at the end of a bird's digestive tract responsible for reproductive and excretory activity.

Commensalism: A relationship between two species in which one benefits and the other neither benefits nor is harmed.

Contour feathers: The exterior feathers of the bird, including the wings and tail.

Diurnal: Active chiefly during the day.

Down: A covering of soft fluffy feathers.

Egg tooth: A sharp projection on the beak that develops in bird embryos. The egg tooth is used by the fledgling to break open the eggshell during hatching and then disappears a few days after birth.

Frugivore: Organism that primarily eats fruit.

Granivore: Organism that feeds mainly on seeds or grains.

Herbivore: Organism that primarily eats plants.

Incubation: The process by which a bird keeps eggs at a temperature suitable for the development of the embryo until they hatch. Usually, birds incubate their eggs by sitting on them.

Insectivore: Organism that primarily eats small insects.

Megapode: A family of large-footed, short-winged birds found in various regions of Australia and Asia. Megapodes do not incubate their eggs using body heat but rather bury their eggs under mounds of warm, decaying vegetation.

Migration: The movement of a bird from one area to another; this movement is usually seasonal, based on a bird's feeding and breeding habits.

Migratory: Refers to a kind of bird that habitually moves from place to place seasonally.

Molting: The process by which a bird loses its feathers and replaces them with a new growth.

Nidicolous: Birds that remain in the nest for a while after hatching.

Nidifugous: Birds that leave the nest shortly after hatching.

Noctural: Active at night.

Omnivore: Organism that eats both plants and animals.

Ornithologist: A scientist who studies the behavior, classification, and physiology of birds.

Parabola: Refers to something that is bowl-shaped. The shape and feathers surrounding an owl's head acts like a parabola, funneling sound into the owl's ear openings.

Parasitism: A relationship between two species in which one benefits at the cost of the other.

Passeriformes: The largest order of birds, which includes about half of the world's species of birds. Passeriformes are true perching birds and are considered to be the most highly evolved of all birds.

Pectoral muscles: The powerful muscles attached to the sternum that gives a bird the strength to fly.

Raptor: A bird of prey, such as an eagle or a hawk.

Rectrices (singular: rectrix): Tail feathers responsible for flight.

Regurgitate: To eject something from the stomach through the mouth.

Remiges (singular: remex): The longest wing feathers on the bird, they are commonly called "flight feathers."

Sedentary: Refers to birds that settle in one area and tend not to move around to other areas (not migratory).

Thoracic ribcage: The bird's ribcage, which protects and encloses the heart, liver and lungs.